The Tree of Partial Knowledge

poems by

Steven R Weiner

Finishing Line Press
Georgetown, Kentucky

My life was a beautiful mystery on the verge of understanding, always on the verge! Think of it!

—Charles Simic, "The World Doesn't End"

The Tree of Partial Knowledge

*For Robin, Catie, and Emily,
They are the first & last lines of everything I am & do,
All beginnings & all promises.*

*And for my second Mom, Arlene Bezark,
For all her love & support, on her 90th birthday*

Copyright © 2023 by Steven R Weiner
ISBN 979-8-88838-229-5 First Edition
All rights reserved under International and Pan-American Copyright Conventions. No part of this book may be reproduced in any manner whatsoever without written permission from the publisher, except in the case of brief quotations embodied in critical articles and reviews.

ACKNOWLEDGMENTS

Thanks are due the following journals where these poems first appeared:

Brief Wilderness, "Returning to Paradise," and "From the Tree of Life."
Glassworks, "Cutting Back the Shoots."
Penmen Review, "Finery and Grace," "Imaging Hearts," and "Psalms Without Trumpets"
Ravens Perch, "HaMelech (The Monarch)"
The American Journal of Poetry, "The Shape of Birth and Death"
Vita Poetica, "A Small World Smaller Yet: a Cenotaph"

Publisher: Leah Huete de Maines
Editor: Christen Kincaid
Cover Art and Design: Steven R Weiner
Author Photo: Steven R Weiner

Order online: www.finishinglinepress.com
also available on amazon.com

Author inquiries and mail orders:
Finishing Line Press
PO Box 1626
Georgetown, Kentucky 40324
USA

Table of Contents

I Am the Night Nurse 1

In The Catskills 2

The Shape of Birth and Death 4

A Field Guide to Birds Who Still Live in The Northeast 6

Imaging Hearts 8

A Small Talk Epiphany 10

Asphalt Beast 12

Returning to Paradise 14

Finery and Grace 15

My Friend Reuben's Garden 16

A Small World Smaller Yet: a Cenotaph 17

In The Opposite of Roadkill 18

In The Dark Aloneness 20

Cutting Back the Shoots 22

Bird In Paper 23

From The Tree of Life 24

A Pomander of Letters 25

Beneath the Tree of Partial Knowledge, It Was Easy
    to Get Lost 27

HaMelech (The Monarch) 29

Psalms Without Trumpets 30

Finally 32

Beyond Our Language, Stars 33

The Sound of Nothing In The Night 36

I Am the Night Nurse

Which means I am the voice at night.
Standing over you, asking how you are,
Did you move your bowels?

I know I can frighten or annoy you with my questions.
Are you breathing? Are you still in pain?
How much, how often, what's the number?
(I have struggled myself with pain,
But only in parentheses, kept private.)

I might ask you if you need something
To help you sleep.
I might wake you, asking.
Because I know what you don't know.
I am the night nurse.
You might wake up at 3 a.m.,
When sleep will be much harder.

I know the night can heal what's broken.
I try to keep my tread light.
But I know that sleeping here will not be easy.
The word hospital
Its badges, labels, numbers, jargon
Hold you in a white thrall.
I hang your medicine. I poke you.

I know when you're scared
And when you're angry,
Some of your secrets.
You'd be surprised what nurses see.
I am here to help you.

I know the night well,
Its routines, its terror.

Crouching at your bedside,
My eyes meeting yours.
I am careful.
I touch your hand and you go back to sleep.
This is my power.

Sleep well, you'll be going home soon.
I'll be here tomorrow.

In The Catskills

When I was a boy
Jews climbed the old trails
To the foothills of the mountains.
It was as close as we could get
To the high camps in the Adirondacks,
So we called them mountains.

That's how summers helped
The Jews of New York City
To survive the troubles
Of this modern life
With electric stoves and color TVs.

I can't forget—I need to thank—
The union contracts
That made TVs and air conditioning,
Newer cars, and quieter summers
Possible for my parents,
United teachers.

We went up to the mountains
On the narrow main roads
Across the new Whitestone
Bridge and through the Bronx
To the main routes through
The middle lands
Where Jews got speeding tickets,
Driving like Jews.

My dad knew how to speak
To country police,
He knew his tools well,
And he knew jokes
Men liked to hear men tell.
This was just like the old country.

These were small towns
Within each colony.
A nickel-gray economy.
It's where cheap classless shtick
Became real comedy.

And everyone knew the tragedies,
The loss of job or grandmother,
The collapse or explosion,
As soon as they landed on us.

It's what people did,
Climb the old trails,
Escape the humidity.
We used the mountains
Like a thermostat
To calm our bodies
And cool our minds.

It was a pilgrimage
With Mah Jong tables
And pinochle decks.
It was no secret.
We loved the gambling.
We loved having small change
We could afford to lose.

The Shape of Birth and Death

I held my crying brother's body when he died
Eight weeks ago, but on this past night
He came to say goodbye—I guess goodbye—
But his only words were *I'm dead*
As if his mind was just beginning to perceive the change.
He died estranged, had not a single person by his side
For years. I can see how hard it must have been
For him to fear death as a leaving,
He had left life behind him long ago,
Lay lost and paralyzed by his enclosed mind.

But now is not the time to describe or assess
These bare naked memories.
There comes a time in every life
To emphasize the common shape
Of a show of life, a cartoon or performance,
Opening and closing—when Porky Pig
Sits laughing when the Looney Tunes hour is ending,
Saying *Th-that's All Folks*
As the black diaphragm closes around him
Engulfing the orange spiral where he cackled till the end
When it swallowed.

A shutter closes on a window or a lens—
That's what it's made to do, named
For the act of shutting, closing the threshold
Where light enters, letting just enough light in.
Or shutting down the cells that take the lights
And shadows and make sense of them.
Not knowing when there is enough light,
Until we see the pictures later, that we've taken.

But the lens of eye and camera is a circle
And our pictures are rectangles, cropped
With artificially sharp angles,
The world laid flat and stretched like a projection
For a map, or a bear or chinchilla skin
To make a fur, to be stylish or keep warm.

Photographs, especially the best ones,
With the best technique or greatest art
Hold the same distortions

As our maps and memories
Where our gaze is cut to the size
And shape of our frames.

Our stories also have their human architecture,
Beginnings, turning points.
Porky Pigs and Daffy Ducks preside at the endings
But the world is a run-on sentence,
A parable whose ending leads to the next parable
Before we have time to attach
A lesson or a question mark,
A comma or a full stop.
My brother lived inside his box.
Procrustes with a butter knife
Could never be a real threat,
But one could only enter at their own risk.
My brother cut everybody else's tongues out,
So they could fit into his square footage.

The lens is circular but our pictures aren't.
The world is round as bellies full of light.
We live inside them.
It's only when we reach the end,
Complete the accidental labyrinth,
Take our last ocean voyage,
That we reach the precipice,
The border of the photograph,
The farthest corner of our map.

Death is the legendary
Monster sailors meet
At the end of their circumnavigation.
And that's where my brother was
In my dream, when I found him,
In the middle of night's forest,
In a roughly oval clearing,
A big fat moon above our heads,
Disappearing as the half-round eyelids
Of the horizon we once shared
Closed around us,
Like a family in a last hug,
Then he left.

A Field Guide to Birds Who Still Live in The Northeast

I have read in the press of the presence of herons and cranes in the wetlands, places in the wild you'd expect a water bird, but these were in metropolitan areas, on the edges of highways and yards, where wetlands can surprise, so the birds will surprise, too, and, likewise, you surprise them.

I have come across wild turkeys and guinea fowl emerging from the tall grasses and low brush at the margins of clusters of young trees, bobbing their graceless necks, and I knew the guineas squawk at the smallest problem, but the turkeys just run, bird heads dipping and nodding with haste, and I know this because it is not unusual to see these odd birds in land cleared for tracts of houses.

You can see hawks above almost any Northeastern highway, and you can hear manic woodpeckers sounding like goosed-up carpenters where there still is wood, drumming for attention or just pecking holes into snags of maple, white birch, stands of aspen, some house walls.

You might also find a demonstration of birds or forensic evidence for their recent life in your binoculars' digital snares, your featherbed, your meditation recorded from nature, or perhaps in your freezer or pot. They are comfortable as parkas or comforters or cushions, and many sound lovely, leaving melodic fragments like molted feathers behind, except for the crows and the jays, and you should know, at least for survival at the end of times, guinea hens and sparrow taste like their respective songs, gamey or delicate, not half bad if you can forget you saw them free and wild.

I hold on to the gentle commotion of their drone and glissando, the soft trill and whistle, birds not named, but noticed, in the morning of an early spring or evening or as a single voice in a neighboring tree when I'm sitting on a stone resting on a hike and I can hear the water churn.

Once, my wife and I observed an entire field of snow geese rise as one white rippling body filling the sky, then settling back down like a knit blanket shaken over a child's bed on our honeymoon when it was colder in October than we realized it would be in Canada, but we found this reservation crowded with white wings, land left for them in someone's will on the outskirts of settled land in Quebec.

I share these facts with you in case you had any doubt that there are still birds in the wild, that the wild still exists on the land between our occupied plots, and we can still, of course, act wildly, use our killing power to meet whatever needs we have, but if you did have doubt, I advise you to hold onto it.

Because nothing about the illusory impermanent presence of birds should remove any of your doubt. In fact, doubt may be one of the most valuable skills any of us can master. I have watched the birds keep one eye open, ready to scatter. They also doubt.

Imaging Hearts

You are in a room where machines chirp
Like chicks in shells who will never peck free,

Machines too sleek and modern
To be birds, with spikes and curling tubes

Arrayed around small screens trained
To display your cells in codes, finding patterns

Of polarized cells and their magnetic
Energy released to move your body.

You are laying on a gurney
Like an old sailor washed up on an island,

Robinson Crusoe being cared for
By a stranger who says she's here to help.

You're stranded on the wild coast of a patient island
Where your blood is the ocean,

Where the sun rises and descends, real or artificial,
You can't tell, white walls surround your island,

On a gurney, where your heart expands and contracts,
Like an old sea lion, its whole body breathes

As one mass, while you run, with the machine,
Up and down the slopes of your pulsations,

The tracings of the muscles of your heart speed up,
Hastened by a need for flight from deep within you,

Afraid of what the doctor thinks is wrong inside,
Or afraid he won't understand it clearly.

No machine knows how to see the constant beating
Your heart and mind have been troubled to imagine.

While your body must decide if it will accept help
And your heart sprints and lunges at your ribs.

The fist in your chest opens, closes, pulls and jerks,
As if by broken habit, lights and shadows fighting with your breath,

A Small Talk Epiphany

My teeth, like the spinning balls of gas
In what's called a universe,
Are slowly drifting apart—
My teeth and my tongue as well,
Drifting further, so far apart
They will be out of reach of conversation,
Too far for any small talk,
And I will become remote and removed
Like some bright new star in the movies,
Some wunderkind of post-pre-surreal illustration,
Some high and mighty priest of hedge funds.

Maybe their mouths are expanding, as well
To make room for their appetites,
Or maybe they're not comfortable
explaining how they could buy a plane
When Jack's only car has been on cinder blocks
For months, rusting and he's out at the job, his manager
Says he's off the crew, been furloughed.
Maybe Miryam next door can explain
How she's working three jobs, raising two kids
By herself since her life partner has been detained
At the border since October.
It can be so easy to say, after long separations,
The hell with it! Numbing the pain with a show of apathy.

My dentist explained how teeth tend to separate
While my mouth was full of bloody spittle, a little tooth debris,
Some mystery compound, mercury-free, and mint-flavored polish,
All produced, extracted, shaped by a crowd of instruments
And a hand moving here and there.
He'd ask me how I was, and I'd grunt through the obstructions
But I didn't mind. My teeth would now be full and shining,
But still expanding, like a galaxy of teeth, I realized, jolted
Enough to disturb the hand that held a drill in my tooth,

So far apart my spreading teeth would free me
From the boring and pointless small talk of daily life—
What's good on Netflix and that jerk in public office,
Freeing me to engage in only the biggest talk,
The fear of death, the fear of living too long,
The fear of saying something wrong and causing pain.

But in that moment of my epiphany,
I could only grunt while he earned his compensation
And the drill echoed like the universe,
As the astronomers have heard it,
Fleeing all its settled dust and stars and planets
In my now otherwise silent propped wide open
Clamped and cotton balled poor mouth
While life outside continued flying round like atoms.
I could hear what sounded like a small plane flying,
My mouth now swelled into a silent scream.

Asphalt Beast

I drive through these empty plains and purposes,
The daily rituals I don't see, but I can call to mind
The work it takes to keep the surrounding fields in good order,
Driving through the tar-black scent of burning oil,
Air as pure as this old motor runs
With its constant coughing.

Black with frost, pale gold with cones
Penetrating from my high beams,
The night goes by, faster than I can see anything,
And at this hour, blind faith does the driving.

It's an asphalt beast we are riding on,
Immune to the carnage of vehicles.
The road rolls back onto its shoulders when it needs rest,
Challenged by the weight of our noisy engines,
As we pass its Scylla and Charybdis.

Massive men moved tons of rock
Exploded into small stones,
To build this road through a notch
In granite mountains, rounded off
By time and rivers of ice,
Crossed by paths used for hunting and trading.
Fields were burned after harvest
To prepare the earth for future crops.
We burned and plowed the fields
To prepare the way for our constant invasions.

But the tricks of navigation have never changed.
We've learned to take the path
That averages the least resistance,
Making the shortest time through the grand landscape.
Crews of migrants and natives, some without papers,
Carved this road through the mountains.
Where are they now? I've heard they're scattered
Like rocks from these overhangs.

Most of these drivers are just going back and forth
Between their work and their other troubles,
Both conquerors and the conquered.

I am driving between somewhere and somewhere else.
Riding this asphalt beast takes all my care.
Outside my cracked glass and metal skin,
Wind was buzzing, being wind.
Another engine, next to mine,
Moves closer than the summer night, and passes,
As we drive from madness to madness,
Looking for a quiet field, a peaceful ocean.

Returning to Paradise

One man on a silver seat,
Chains descending from a creaking frame,
The sounds of playgrounds—
Child running on an old man's knees.

He swings from the low seat, spine vertical
To the high and horizontal
Flight of reason,
Trying to be begin again, to forget
His earthbound thoughts and aging lessons.

He shifts his weight,
Narrows his focus
To the swing, the pumping rhythm,
Kicks up his legs from underneath
With a push against the concrete.

And his body rises,
He flows, he tilts, he fidgets, resists, stretches
Out his legs into the distance,

Then he descends,
And kicks back up again
      Propelling his body
                To a new height
Above this paradise
From his early years,
The chains now rusted.

He looks down,
    Kicks back,
        Swings forward in a downward arc,
Swings back up again,
    Past the familiar
        Into the unseen,
                Backwards.

Finery and Grace

There was a thin dignified
Upright old lady
At the front counter—
You know the type—they gather
In churches and other sanctuaries—
Paying for her toast and tea with small change.
I wondered what she meant by saying
"I was up late watching the moon
Mending its silver-haired cloud finery
With the thinnest needle of light.
I sewed the grace back in."
I wanted to ask her, but she didn't wait.
I thought, with all the shit we're standing in
These chilly, broken days,
How could anyone think like that,
Let alone say it while they were counting
Out nickels and pennies?
Maybe I didn't hear it right,
But it would be much too strange
To have imagined anything like that.
It was plain daylight.
No one could conjure up such mystic balderdash
With the sun glaring on every
Little bit of human labor
In our hemisphere, but then
It had probably been plain moonlight
When she took out her sewing kit,
An old Schrafft's Candy box.
Metal, hinged, the way the best candy came
When she was first learning how to sew.
I thought all day about what she might have said.
About her and the moon and the way they dressed,
Not rich at all, but dignified, simple.
Defiant with her self-respect.
She stood upright.

My Friend Reuben's Garden

Watching him work
Throughout the growing season
And even before, preparing.
I grow

Curious, about the rain,
The sprouts of truth, his garden,
Vines spread. He tended soil,
Rich and moist, not worry free.

He pulled weeds, aligned rows
With Buddhist prayer flags
And a fence, keeping ticks,
Blights, and aphids
Away, a small distance.
On his face, A smile grew
beneath rimless glasses,
Sweat-bright, gray-fringed, Jewish friend,
Who worries about death
While he serves life in his garden.

The universe may be less
Random, sometimes kind
Where soil is prepared
For vegetables and flowers,
Shovels turning over
The illusions of solid earth
Unbedding the elements of soil
And shaking chance awake.
Something will grow—
At least one tomato,
A lot of weeds,
Surely a blossom of squash.

The string bearing eight prayer flags
Between deer fencing shakes
The printed red and blue and yellow fabric.
One flag unfurls in the wind,
You see, it flaps over the garden,
A sign of his devotion,
A different kind of prayer.

A Small World Smaller Yet: a Cenotaph

from obituaries in The New York Times of people who died from infection with covid-19

The barber and his scissors died.
What she did was read, & draw, and read some more.
A hummingbird & puppeteer, she flapped her own wings.
He never left the neighborhood, but they had to bury him.
She had that sense of duty, still alive.
Famous for his cake, he added rum.

One of four in a quartet, he played the cello at their side.
She was a chaplain offering psalms to prisoners.
Two magicians cut in half, one not coming back.
A small nun in a small order, her stature rose with acts of love.
He sold encyclopedias and collected reference books, he knew.
She changed her mind a hundred times, but always fought for what seemed right to her.

She named her daughter Poet, what more could I say?
Black and beautiful, not an easy life, she showed students how to make a film.
He loved the discipline and luxury of mathematics, the equations of justice.
Most of the words she knew unspoken yet, she hitchhiked to Nice instead.
He had a gift like Michelangelo's for sports, but never made a masterpiece.
She found a lot of hatred, but tried to shed it at her door.

A piano at his back, a welder's torch in front of him.
She climbed mountains and fixed kidneys and life flowed through her hands.
He became a movie star, with his violin.
The steel-pan was his instrument, his home was in the metal notes.
Their passion was repairing things, and they knew how to cook.
A genius in math and magic who found a safe home in a puzzle world.

He photographed museum art, beauty copied beautifully.
A researcher with golden hands, she coaxed her results out of tubes.
He studied mosquitoes and found some good in them.
She liked raspberries the most.

In The Opposite of Roadkill

The civilized are crushed
And flattened by the semi-wild
Who have adjusted to our dominance

Grown wild
By growing wildly
In vineyards and green pastures
No deity has trampled.

What has been crushed
Are not grapes
But organs we have coughed up
At the impact of a virus

In the size and shape
Of another universe
Trying to devour.

I don't mean to terrify,
But fear is sometimes needed

Even if it's wanted less
Than a caller who collects debts.

A little after five,
A call interrupts you
From another world
You've never known
Saying, "We're here to repossess you."

So you put a mask on
To protect yourself,
But you will never
Cross the road again
Or take a deep breath
The way you did once,

And every time you see a fox
Or possum or racoon
With its flesh exposed
For all the worlds to see

You could understand
A little more of how

it came to be there,
Crushed and renamed
Or how this tragedy
Allows a family of crows
To live another day

In our world
Where the civilized
Write poems about fragility
And think that might save us.

In The Dark Aloneness

While night and snow
In glistened hours and clustered flakes
Pass the time,
I watch from inside,
the inches, speed of wind
And pressure, pushing mercury
Up its thin tube,
So we can read the air,
Measure its mystery.

The snow isn't falling as fast
As the wind propels it into us
Like nails of ice
Driven into our freezing skin,
Through the silver gray of breath,
Riveting the dark
Planks against our windows
Easier to see ourselves reflected.
Now we don't want to look.

In the naked body
Of my house there is a skeleton
Of wood and plastic
Bones that jest with us by creaking
As if they could break soon,
Shifting just enough
To make it possible
For socks to roll downhill
And the walls to divide space
Making rooms to hide our bodies.

I don't want to be responsible
For what someone might see in me
The way I've wounded them,
The ways the world's been wounded,

I don't want the window glass and insulation.
I want the heat and cold and moderation
Swirling all around me.
I don't want a table of the tides,
Or trains or Sunday dinners

With the entire family
Who have never really known
The dark world, the secret puzzle,
And the jigsaw inside me,
Nor the frost that heaved my skin
Into the silly mask
I wear when you are watching.

Cutting Back The Shoots

To the lost and to the last loves
In their gardens, who evicted me,
I would send these flowers—

White foxglove, pink columbine,
Days past their peak bloom,

Sprawling unkempt as a drunken guest
Across the little grove
I keep privately.

Seeds taken by the night birds,
Final blossoms spent

While the lost love,
That defended soul,
Who still needs nothing I can give,
Finds her respite where she can.

My last love, the most recent one,
I may never try again,
Has her own seeds,
Flowers she insisted on.
She needs even less from me.

This is mine to keep
Within this sturdy fence,
Safe from deer, for swallowtails,
For bumblers, for me
And the wandering sphinx moth.

The garden needs to be pruned,
Blooms of no more use to me,
And I have shears.

Bird In Paper

If I folded you
In half
Along a freehand line
And folded you
Again in two
Bending up one corner here,
One corner there,
Into wings,
My origami lover,
Would you fly
Or sit there, folded
Arms between us, claiming
You were not
A leaf of paper,
You were not my bird,
You would still be mine
And you will know me.

From The Tree of Life

Worn down by touch,
Hanging slack from my shoulders
Like two empty nets,
These two hands hold fruit,
A life that's sliced in half, some
Damage has been done
Although the blade was sharp
As a lonely day,
Sharp enough
To slit a kosher throat. Juice
Squeezed out by the pressure
Of the blade
Drips on the table
Cloth, and spreads
A yellow stain but some
Mistakes can't be avoided.
At least there is no heart
Or arteries to squeeze the blood
Faster. Fruit's a way
Life grows within a season,
Ripens fast but dies slow
As a seed on stone,
So when you take a bite
You taste the sugar,
As precious as any sacrifice
Offered to a god,
Or what we demand
From those we love most.

A Pomander of Letters

While you walk, my love across the intervening space
We do not have as much time
Left to anticipate, remember.

We live within the walls we've built,
The drawers we've filled,
The sheds and bedrooms.
I remember the unfolded couch
In a Point Judith motel
Where we sagged into the middle of the bed,
Into each other,
And held onto the edges of the mildewed frame,
As if we would drown into the other,
As if we realized we were meant to sleep together.

We feared our instincts,
That creature of poor habits who reacts
With pride and anger and the defensiveness
Of a thin-walled hollow ball of smoke and ash
Burned down to tears so long ago,
The same fella who made us reach
Our hands out and discover.

I am not as quick, nor steady
On my feet as I was
When I first began to watch you
Cross the space between
"I think you're cute"
And "I love you."

There is a vast difference
Between a letter about love
About how hard it was, and is,
To navigate that space between two skins
That touch sometimes, not always,

And a love letter full of promises
We recognized and skirted,
The electricity of friction, passions rubbed
Against each other, burning sparklers
I saved in boxes when they burned out, our eternity.

I stored a stack of sworn love,
Tied with a velvet ribbon,
As a pomander to fill the spaces
In my chest-- it's now our chest,
With a scent we can imagine
Even now, when love has aged well.

Beneath the Tree of Partial Knowledge, It Was Easy to Get Lost

I left home, my chest behind one of my father's old ties, broad with a weather-beaten pattern, my eyes under his brown fedora, with my versions of his smile and his blue-gray eyes that looked beyond me

Until midnight, when everyone had vanished from his sight, leaving us with awkward love, he needed me to laugh and listen, but that's when I learned that one day everyone will be gone.

He taught me how to fix things, how to find the broken parts, unseen beneath the typing, ticking, working pieces, and watching from a distance, I could still see I was lucky, but I'd fixed so much by feel, for so long, everything my fingers touched felt broken.

I learned his stubborn nature, tried again, but I was worn down, as stones are worn by water, and plowshares dulled by stubborn earth, but rocks will roll on and the horse will pull, and with enough glue, dried transparent, everything will look whole.

Life was brought to me by chance and with persistence I could thrive, but I subsided. I need another chance to grow up. I was injured, more than once, my knee against a cinder block, my lip against a milkman's box, a batted ball, my father's insults, my mother's gentle teasing, and I grew lost in wounds, in the itch of their slow healing, in the binding and unwinding of the gauze.

I could not imagine being found but if I was saved, I must have been discarded first, my tribe disbanding just as I joined, so I wandered, found a path changed by the taking. Sometimes I just tossed myself onto the next stone, moving forward without progress.

Where was I when I tried and failed so often I succeeded and I felt completely lost, only to find recently that I had often been successful as a child? Was it my imagination or my memory that failed me?

I began where I had started, on the side streets, avoiding the boulevards and the boulevardiers, who seemed to know everything because they were so well-groomed. They knew less than I did.

I began at the beginning of the rootless vine of partial knowledge, the tree where winter was sleep, and the air was still as life, where life waits, dancing thither, dancing yon, across the distance between sundown red and sunrise red where light and shadow turn the massive heights into thin silhouettes, and mystery becomes another word for the trickery of distance.

Of all the memories and objects I could have kept, I kept my distance, expected nothing more than keeping what they gave me.

There were days when I was under sea a few weeks, driftwood diving underneath and through insistent tides, sea-bones cracked like nervous knuckles, and the vapor fill the sky with mist around the monuments of ships and slaves and fools and traders, soldiers, priests and saints and horses, did I tell you I was lost?

But I danced with twigs, the awkward dance of time with wood, the sweep of breezes, the orchestra of things and beings. They bewildered, I was left in basket and in cradle, and when I wanted more than food, I was left with milk in bottles, tamed before I had a chance to run through mountains, but I became familiar with the zoos.

I grew up in solitude that fed me, gave me cake and wine and endless rumination, but then I learned to fix what's broken, how to heal wounds, cover lesions, but then I saw that gluing cracks and replacing springs doesn't mean the thing will work well, and when I found my way, I saw how many times I crossed my own path.

I wish I could make room for a more peaceful way of knowing nothing, learning more, accumulating knowledge from experience, know for sure how I've grown since I was born, where I am going.

I'm tired of the broken wheels and scattered parts, the dented milk boxes, the scars and stigma, glue and bindings, I must know everything. It's all still broken. I meander.

HaMelech (The Monarch)

Forgive me my oversight,
The stubborn ways I never notice
You, a Monarch among butterflies
With designs for a universe
Drawn with black ink on your yellow wings
The size of a child's palm--
You, who rose from a caterpillar's bed,
A Sabbath rest, a contemplation,
Can now fly.
But you come to rest
On my finger.

In this haven, where butterflies
Are kept safe, and we mingle,
You touch me with the grace of dew
On morning's ragged shawl.
I am drab and earthbound,
Clothed in the colors of stone and sand.
It makes it hard for me to greet you.
My hand trembles.
So I close my eyes,
But the act of closing doesn't soothe me.

I open my eyes.
You were waiting.
I am your perch.
You are my miracle.
We stand together
Like tree and cradle.
My hands flutter,
Your wings shake,
But for one long minute,
We are steadfast.
And maybe, we are both amazed.

Psalms Without Trumpets

The music of barely singing
Is hard to write,
Can scarcely be heard
Like voices rising from green wood,
Shy smoke mixing with the steam,
A little sibilance behind the daily buzzing
Like harmonics so subtle that you can't hear
Them, but the sound's so full and rich
Or thin as a battered tea kettle's
Rattle, but it once did whistle
And it knew how it was meant to sound.

These psalms, The kind
that gather silently from behind
the lips of those who used to sing
But now pray only out of habit or desperation
Are the most devout because they grew
inside hearts that had been shuttered
And this vague hum, a pulse of wishes,
The murmur of intentions before the acts
that follow and now both are free,
The wish and power.
That's where the humming
Of the Psalms come from,
Wires filled with energy that need an outlet,
Ears like a retriever or a hound
Looking for the wounded
May be more sensitive to prayer.
How many of us pray to be heard
When we really need to listen?

We always suspected something
Was being hidden in our sleep,
Some dream of a better life,
When things within ourselves
And beyond our block were different.

I have listened
Like I listen to the pulse of rivers
For the hint in the air of psalms
First spoken, Not blasted

through the trumpets
Of the would be angels.
No, the sounds I hear
Below the breath, Between
The warbles and the hiding,
The pause between noise's absence
And a sky full of static
Are harder than silence to record:

The end of a lullaby,
Rain's slow descent,
The tides in their resting phase,
A flute between notes,
Small paws in the underbrush,
A flap of wings,
A pause to catch breath,
A flounder shifting in sand,
The sound of a dream half asleep,
Goldberg reciting to God,
The psalms without trumpets,
The praise of the oceans and skies,
An egg hatching,
The twentieth shovel of dirt,
A bowl and a pitcher,
Washing hands,
The last chords on a 45.

We whisper praises.
We sing with our silence.
We praise with our whispers
As if something was sleeping,
And we wanted to let it sleep.

Finally

In the aspiring light,
Bedeviled by birdsongs,
The noise of the nested,
Dreams tried to achieve form.

My hands, after the morning chill,
Grew warmer with the day's use,
And I reached out with them,
Flexed my arms, extended them,
To hold tools, a pen,
And an Agatha Christie to lean on.

Some scrap paper,
The other side I used
For an old list of errands,
Where I wrote lines and verses
And then I replaced them.

I watched the light change.
I tried to invoke it
With just words.
But I kept missing something.
I didn't know, the phases
As the tinge of yellow grew
Then grew colder, pale white.

In the expiring twilight,
My restless thoughts struggled
Like a cranky toddler
Writhing in his father's arms.
Thoughts of fortunes
Never won or now exhausted,
Settled with me into the hour's nest,
And we became calm.

Beyond Our Language, Stars

What amazes me most is how
A sky of roaring furnaces can stay mute.
When one star dies one more ignites
To take its place, both soundless
As if a smith had struck his anvil--
Dull silver as a winter sky,
But it didn't ring like iron, like a church bell,
It just glowed, throwing sparks out like a river
Into silence, making stars.

The crowd of celestial balls of flame is lush,
But greeted by a sparse few in a dark space,
Where every image stands in
For something else we wanted
To explore, draw out some mystery
Nearby and make it ours.

We say the night is pitch-black
Though light leaks everywhere,
From stars as constant as the blue,
Where a galaxy of crows
Is showered by the down shed
From a nebula of white doves.

We're all deaf,
Or they're all mute,
Or we don't recognize their language.

But there is no peace.
The night and day
Of our experience
Are no use.
Light argues constantly
With dark matter
Which we can't see
But we feel ghosts.

In a sky as huge as midnight,
We know only
What we don't know.
We struggle to extend our sight

With scopes and cameras.
We catch a hint or two
But nothing clear as daylight in the hush.

The only noise comes as we focus,
Rub our thumbs against the knurled knobs.
Tubes squeak like cooing doves.
As we adjust, we magnify
The magnificent to fit our maps,
Our specks of cardboard.

Our eyes turn up to the speckles,
The multitude of multitudes above,
A hundred million holes
Poked into our jar lid.
Like Moses with a view of God,
We see much more than we can absorb.

But it keeps our mouths from small talk.
Hours pass. With extra care,
We tuck our children into their beds.

On a distant axis, stars twist
And turn on the scale of legends
Beyond senses.
Thoughts of sleep, aware of starlight
Engender thoughts of time and distance
Way past the cooing and the caws
Of creatures we cannot imagine
But our eyes still reach
For something to illuminate their songs.

The stars we see are long dead,
And the new light
Will never find us.
What we call new is so much older,
With more perils than we ever could
Know well..

We shy away from awe,
Preferring knowledge,

Using what we know to capture
An image of the unknown we can keep
Until the morning
When we tell our children
Stories of a few stars, we selected
So they believe the universe will welcome them,
And their children's generations.

The Sound of Nothing in the Night

I go out in some late hours
To my front porch, just to listen.
Where I love to hear—whatever comes,
A late bird, village traffic, sometimes.
If you asked me what was there,
I'd answer, *nothing*.
Meaning, nothing much,
Nothing that demands description,
Nothing to the gaze,

But then I'd say I listen
To nothing as it skims the trees.
You feel a rustle, hear vibration
Of feathers falling into reeds,
And even that is too specific
For the slow rush you hear,
Gifted the green sound of plants
Brushing down the air,
Becomes a wind that churns the branches,
Finds a rhythm there,
And becomes breezes.

Blowing air, however rough or gently,
Carries heard and unheard prayers
Through the twilight
To the absolute
Light or dark.

Yud, hay, vuv, hay—
That's how we spell
God's name in Hebrew
And that's what I hear as the green plants
Sway and chant vespers
With a constant whisper
Of being and becoming,
As the dark digs in.
And the trunks and branches respond.
They offer amen.

www.ingramcontent.com/pod-product-compliance
Lightning Source LLC
Chambersburg PA
CBHW022123090426
42743CB00008B/985